★ *GREAT SPORTS TEAMS* ★

THE SAN FRANCISCO

49ERS

FOOTBALL TEAM

Arlene Bourgeois Molzahn

Enslow Publishers, Inc.

40 Industrial Road	PO Box 38
Box 398	Aldershot
Berkeley Heights, NJ 07922	Hants GU12 6BP
USA	UK

http://www.enslow.com

To Mark, my computer expert

Library of Congress Cataloging-in-Publication Data

Molzahn, Arlene Bourgeois.
    The San Francisco 49ers football team / Arlene Bourgeois Molzahn.
       p. cm. — (Great sports teams)
    Includes bibliographical references and index.
    Summary: Surveys the history of the San Francisco 49ers professional football team, covering key players and coaches as well as some of the team's great games.
    ISBN 0-7660-1280-8
    1. San Francisco 49ers (Football team) Juvenile literature. [1. San Francisco 49ers (Football team)—History. 2. Football—History.] I. Title. II. Series.
GV956.S3M65   2000
796.332′64′0979461—dc21   99-38675
                                          CIP

Printed in the United States of America

10 9 8 7 6 5 4 3 2 1

To Our Readers: All Internet addresses in this book were active and appropriate when we went to press. Any comments or suggestions can be sent by e-mail to Comments@enslow.com or to the address on the back cover.

Illustration Credits: AP/Wide World Photos.

Cover Illustration: AP/Wide World Photos.

Cover Description: Steve Young (left) and Brent Jones celebrate a touchdown.

CONTENTS

*R*oger Craig takes the handoff from Joe Montana. Craig played in three Super Bowls as a member of the 49ers.

SUPER BOWL XXIII

On January 22, 1989, Joe Robbie Stadium in Miami, Florida, was filled with 75,129 supercharged fans. The San Francisco 49ers and the Cincinnati Bengals were meeting to decide which team would win Super Bowl XXIII and claim the Vince Lombardi Trophy.

The Rematch

Coach Sam Wyche had led his American Football Conference (AFC) champion Bengals to 12 wins and 4 losses. Led by Coach Bill Walsh, the 49ers were National Football Conference (NFC) champions, with a season record of 10 wins and 6 losses. Both teams won their first two playoff games. Sportswriters labeled the game a rematch, because both teams played in Super Bowl XVI, with the 49ers winning that game by a score of 26–21.

On the Monday before the Super Bowl, fans in San Francisco became very concerned about the team's outstanding wide receiver, Jerry Rice. He had suffered an ankle injury early in the season, and now he had turned his ankle in practice. But much to their relief, his ankle recovered enough for him to be in the starting lineup on Super Bowl Sunday.

Fallen Soldiers

The game started slowly. The 49ers received the opening kickoff. After only a few plays into the first quarter, Steve Wallace, offensive tackle for the 49ers, suffered a broken leg. A short time later, the fans in Joe Robbie Stadium again became very quiet. Tim Krumrie, the leading tackler for the Bengals, also suffered a broken leg and was carted off the field.

Near the end of the first quarter, 49ers kicker Mike Cofer booted a 41-yard field goal, and the quarter ended 49ers 3, Bengals 0.

The second quarter was scoreless until 1:15 remained in the half, when the Bengals kicker Jim Breech booted a 34-yard field goal making the score 3–3 at halftime.

The Bengals received the kickoff to start the third quarter. Their 9-minute drive ended with a 43-yard field goal, which put the Bengals ahead by 3. With 50 seconds left in the third quarter, the 49ers intercepted a pass and kicked a 32-yard field goal. The score was tied, 6–6. With 34 seconds left in the third quarter, Stanford Jennings of the Bengals took the kickoff and ran 93 yards for the first touchdown in the game. The third quarter ended with the score Bengals 13, 49ers 6.

Tied Up

Early in the fourth quarter, Joe Montana began an 85-yard drive for the San Francisco 49ers, which ended with a 14-yard touchdown pass to Jerry Rice. The extra point tied the score, 13–13.

With 3:20 left to play, Cincinnati took the lead for the third time. Breech kicked a 40-yard field goal, to make the score Bengals 16, 49ers 13.

The 49ers got the ball back on their own 8-yard line with only 3:12 left to play.

"Let's go, be tough," Montana commanded.[1] Then he methodically moved his team downfield with a combination of passes and running plays.

With only 39 seconds left, the 49ers still needed ten yards to score a touchdown. Montana spotted John Taylor in the end zone. Taylor, who had dropped the only ball thrown to him earlier in the game, caught Montana's 10-yard touchdown pass. The extra point made the score 49ers 20, Bengals 16. A few seconds later, the 49ers were celebrating in the locker room. San Francisco had won its third Super Bowl in seven years.

After the game, Bengals coach Sam Wyche said, "The injury was crucial to us. When we lost Tim [Krumrie], we lost our best tackler . . . "[2]

When asked about his ankle, Jerry Rice, the game's Most Valuable Player (MVP), said, "It really was sore early in the week. But there was no way it was going to keep me out of the Super Bowl."[3]

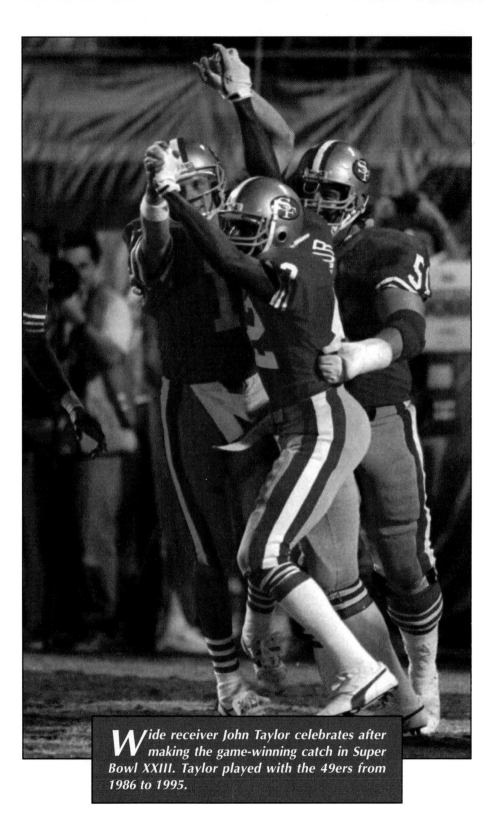

*W*ide receiver John Taylor celebrates after making the game-winning catch in Super Bowl XXIII. Taylor played with the 49ers from 1986 to 1995.

*J*erry Rice was named the Most Valuable Player of Super Bowl XXIII. In that game, Rice caught 11 passes for 215 yards.

Super Feeling

In the winning locker room, a happy Randy Cross, center for the 49ers, told reporters, "Finally after twenty-three years, the Super Bowl is super."[4]

Many football fans agree that Super Bowl XXIII was one of the most exciting Super Bowls ever played.

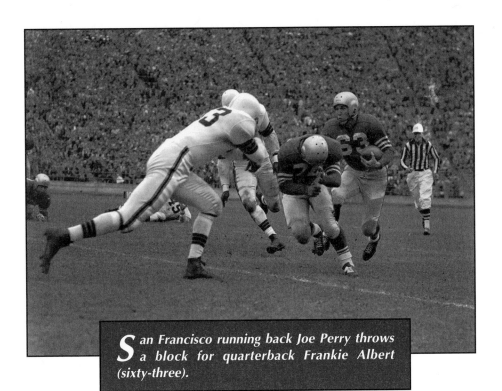

*S*an Francisco running back Joe Perry throws a block for quarterback Frankie Albert (sixty-three).

2

AN EXCITING HISTORY

nthony J. "Tony" Morabito, a partner in a San Francisco lumber business, tried to obtain a National Football League (NFL) franchise for San Francisco. After his efforts failed, he and several partners decided to form a team outside the established league. In 1946, the San Francisco 49ers became a charter member of the All-America Football Conference (AAFC). Morabito immediately began searching for players on established NFL teams. He offered them contracts with large salaries. He signed the best college players in California. He hired Lawrence "Buck" Shaw of Santa Clara University to coach the team.

AAFC

Morabito rented Kezar Stadium for the team's home games. Now, because of Morabito's efforts, the city of San Francisco had its own football team.

In 1947, Morabito bought out his original partners and shared ownership of the team with his brother Vic Morabito.

The 49ers had winning records during the four years they were in the AAFC. Several players were recognized for their outstanding play during those years. Among them was their quarterback Frankie Albert, who was named co-MVP of the league in 1948.

The Merger

In 1949, people were not going to many AAFC games. Since the people were not paying to see the games, the owners were losing a lot of money. The AAFC was also causing hardships for the NFL by drafting many good college players and offering them large contracts. In 1950, the two leagues agreed to merge. Four teams from the AAFC were accepted in the NFL: the San Francisco 49ers, the Cleveland Browns, the Baltimore Colts, and the Brooklyn–New York Yankees. The Yankees disbanded in 1951.

The first few years in the NFL were disappointing ones for the 49ers and their fans. In fact, it was not until 1970, 1971, and 1972 that the 49ers finished first in their division. However, they were never able to win the NFC championship game.

In 1977, Edward DeBartolo, Sr., purchased the team and then turned it over to his son Eddie DeBartolo, Jr., the league's youngest owner. DeBartolo, Jr., immediately began working toward his goal of having a winning football team for San Francisco. "Eddie is very committed to winning," said former 49ers quarterback

The San Francisco 49ers Football Team

Joe Montana. "You have to put forth money to produce a team. Eddie did that."[1]

DeBartolo, Jr., Turns Things Around

During the first two years under DeBartolo, Jr.'s, ownership, the team's record was 7 wins and 23 losses. Then DeBartolo hired Bill Walsh as head coach in 1979. With Walsh's installment of what became known as the West Coast Offense, a decade of brilliance began. From 1979 to 1988, Coach Walsh's teams won Super Bowls XVI, XIX, and XXIII. The 49ers became known as the Team of the Decade for the 1980s.

Quarterback Joe Montana said of Walsh, "What set the coach apart was his knowledge of the game. He

Hugh McElhenny (thirty-nine) led all NFL running backs in yards per carry in 1952 and 1954.

*R*onnie Lott jars the ball free from Miami Dolphins receiver Mark Clayton with this bone-crushing hit. Lott was one of the most dominant defensive backs of the 1980s.

was always analyzing and coming up with new things."[2]

Walsh retired after Super Bowl XXIII, and his defensive coordinator, George Seifert, was hired as head coach.

Of DeBartolo's choice for head coach, Walsh said, "Seifert is an excellent technician and taskmaster. He has a gifted mind and is extremely well organized."[3]

A Smooth Transition

DeBartolo had made the right choice. During his rookie year as head coach, Seifert guided the 49ers to a victory in Super Bowl XXIV.

After the Super Bowl XXIV victory, Seifert gave credit to Walsh: "It has really been the strength of Bill's personality, his demands and his intelligence, and the structure that he established and the people he hired that have enabled us to do all this."[4]

Seifert led his teams to winning seasons during each of his eight years as head coach of the 49ers. His coaching career was highlighted by victories in both Super Bowls XXIV and XXIX.

In 1997, a new era began for the San Francisco 49ers when Steve Mariucci became their head coach.

*K*nown for being a fierce hitter, Leo Nomellini was one of the 49ers stars of the early days.

STAR PLAYERS

A number of 49ers have been elected to the Pro Football Hall of Fame. In 1969, Leo Nomellini was the first to receive that honor. Joe Perry, Hugh McElhenny, Y. A. Tittle, John Henry Johnson, Bob St. Clair, Jimmy Johnson, Joe Montana, Dave Wilcox, Ronnie Lott, and Head Coach Bill Walsh followed. Recent players such as Jerry Rice and Steve Young will surely be in the Hall of Fame someday.

Leo Nomellini

When the San Francisco 49ers joined the NFL in 1950, their first draft pick was Leo Nomellini. Nomellini played offensive and defensive tackle. He excelled at rushing the quarterback on defense and at opening holes for the runners on offense. He played in every 49ers game for fourteen seasons, and he saw action in 174 consecutive league games. Nomellini played in six Pro Bowls, receiving All-Pro honors four times on defense and twice on offense. He earned the nickname Leo the Lion.

Tony Canadeo, a Hall of Fame running back with the Green Bay Packers, remembered, "When you played against Nomellini, you knew one of the reasons why he was known as the Iron Man of football."[1]

Joe Perry

Joe Perry was one of the fastest running backs ever to play in the NFL. He became known as the Jet after Frankie Albert, San Francisco 49ers quarterback, said, "I've never seen anybody get such a fast start. He's strictly jet-propelled."[2]

With his blazing speed, Perry would explode in the middle of the line for great yardage. He was the first back in NFL history to gain more than a thousand yards in two consecutive seasons, 1953 and 1954. Upon retirement, Perry ranked second only to former Cleveland star Jim Brown in lifetime yards rushing. Perry had a great ability to understand and remember plays. He knew the assignment for each player. When his quarterback would need a breather, Perry played that position. He was inducted into the Pro Football Hall of Fame in 1969.

Joe Montana

Joe Montana, who played for the 49ers from 1979 to 1992, will be remembered as one of the league's greatest quarterbacks. He became known as the Comeback Kid because he guided the 49ers to 31 fourth-quarter come-from-behind wins in his career. He earned the nickname Joe Cool because of the poise he showed when his team was behind.

The San Francisco 49ers Football Team

Coach Bill Walsh of the 49ers said, "When the game is on the line and you need someone to go in there and win it, I would rather have Joe Montana than anyone else who ever played the game."[3]

During his fourteen years with the 49ers, Montana led his team to four Super Bowl victories. He was voted the Most Valuable Player of the Super Bowl a

*J*oe Montana is one of the greatest quarterbacks in NFL history. He led the 49ers to four Super Bowl titles.

record three times. In 1989 and 1990 he was voted the league's MVP.

Roger Craig

Roger Craig was a 49ers running back for eight years. He helped them win three Super Bowls and was selected to the All-Pro team four times. In 1985, he became the first player in NFL history to gain over 1,000 yards rushing and 1,000 yards receiving in the same season.

Jerry Rice

Jerry Rice was the first-round draft choice of the 49ers in 1985. He had a constant desire to improve his game. He soon became one of the greatest pass receivers in the NFL. Rice's outstanding play for the 49ers was an important factor in the victories of Super Bowls XXIII, XXIV, and XXIX. He was named the MVP of Super Bowl XXIII.

Former NFL quarterback and TV analyst Pat Haden said of Rice, "In my estimation, Jerry Rice is the best player ever to play the game. He has made every play imaginable, short plays, long plays, clutch plays, acrobatic plays, easy plays, postseason plays, and he plays exceptionally well in big games."[4]

Steve Young

In 1991, when Steve Young replaced Joe Montana at quarterback, many fans were skeptical. But Young quickly showed his critics that he had outstanding leadership ability, great mobility under pressure, and an accurate throwing arm. He was the highest-rated

*S*teve Young replaced Joe Montana as the 49ers starting quarterback, and led them to victory in Super Bowl XXIX. Young was named the game's MVP.

passer in the NFL from 1991 to 1994, and again in 1996 and 1997. He was named the NFL's MVP in 1992 and 1994. He led his team to victory in Super Bowl XXIX and was named the MVP of that game as well.

Young's opponents recognized his abilities. George Dyer, defensive coordinator for the Los Angeles Rams, once called Young "a defensive coach's nightmare."[5]

Tim Green, a defensive end for the Atlanta Falcons, once said, "When you have to play Young, you wake up with a sickening feeling."[6]

*E*ddie DeBartolo, Jr., took over control of the
49ers in 1977. He helped turn them into a
football powerhouse.

BUILDING THE TEAM

Fans of the San Francisco 49ers can look back and identify several people who made a huge difference in their team's history. Their founder, Tony Morabito, made tremendous efforts and took financial chances in 1946 when he established the team. Much credit must also be given to Lawrence "Buck" Shaw, the team's first coach. Each of the four years his 49ers were in the AAFC, they finished second to the Cleveland Browns.

After the AAFC championship game of 1949, Shaw said, "Four years ago I'd never met Paul Brown. Now I scheme to beat him, dream of beating him, and wind up screaming because I haven't beaten him."[1]

Buck Shaw

The record of the 49ers was good enough for San Francisco to be accepted into the NFL in 1950 when the two leagues merged. Shaw remained coach of the

49ers from 1950 to 1954. His best NFL record came in 1953, when his team went 9–3, finishing second in the league. In 1954, his backfield consisted of future Hall of Famers Y. A. Tittle, Joe Perry, and Hugh McElhenny. John Henry Johnson, another Hall of Famer who had his best years with the Pittsburgh Steelers, was also a member of that backfield. This backfield became known as one of the best in pro football history.

Eddie DeBartolo, Jr.

Much of the 49ers' success must be credited to Eddie DeBartolo, Jr. Soon after he became the owner of the club, he and his staff began searching for personnel who would bring championships to San Francisco. He also developed a good relationship with his players.

"I really enjoyed playing for him," former All-Pro defensive end Fred Dean said. "I always felt good in his environment. To me, he was just a great owner."[2]

After some legal problems, DeBartolo, Jr., gave up control of the team in the late 1990s.

Bill Walsh

In 1979, Bill Walsh was hired as head coach and general manager of the team, which had finished the previous year with 2 wins and 14 losses.

Walsh said, "When I became head coach, I looked for assistants who were creative and open to new ideas. I never wanted our team to stand still."[3]

Walsh began installing an offensive game plan that became known as the West Coast Offense. Walsh's new offense was soon put into the playbooks of many

*B*ill Walsh (with Joe Montana) was named head coach in 1979. Coaches around the league still use his offensive strategy which came to be known as the West Coast Offense.

teams in the NFL. In 1981, his third year as head coach, his team won Super Bowl XVI. He also led his teams to wins in Super Bowl XIX in 1984 and Super Bowl XXIII in 1988.

Bill Walsh is also known for developing great quarterbacks, such as Pro Football Hall of Famer Dan Fouts in San Diego, Ken Anderson in Cincinnati, and Joe Montana and Steve Young while they were with the 49ers. Bill Walsh will be remembered as the genius who coached the 1980s Team of the Decade.

George Seifert

George Seifert, who at one time worked as an usher for the San Francisco games at Kezar Stadium, joined

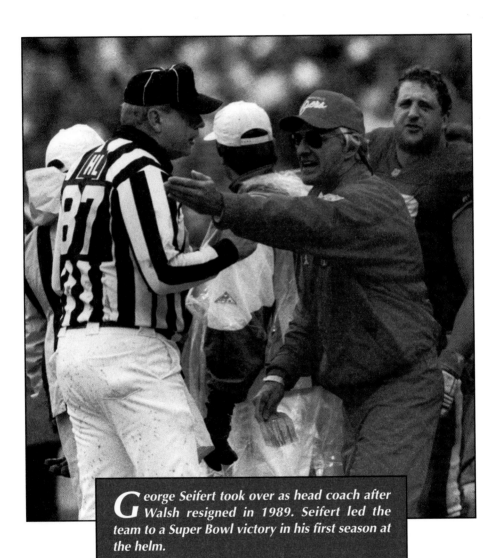

George Seifert took over as head coach after Walsh resigned in 1989. Seifert led the team to a Super Bowl victory in his first season at the helm.

the 49ers in 1980 as a secondary coach under Bill Walsh. He was promoted to defensive coordinator in 1983. In his second season with the team, the 49ers won Super Bowl XVI. During his years as defensive coordinator, his teams finished at or near the top in all the NFL's defensive categories. He followed Bill Walsh as head coach in 1989.

Of his successor, Walsh said, "George is clearly the brightest mind in the game defensively. He's a dedicated football coach who possesses a great instinct for the game and great command of the technical aspects of the game."[4]

Seifert remained head coach of the 49ers for eight seasons and guided his teams to victories in Super Bowl XXIV and XXIX. He resigned in 1996 after taking the 49ers to the playoffs for five consecutive years.

Dwight Clark leaps to make what turned out to be one of the most well-known catches in football history.

THRILLING MOMENTS

O n January 10, 1982, the Dallas Cowboys played the San Francisco 49ers in the National Football Conference Championship Game for the right to play in Super Bowl XVI.

1982 NFC Championship Game

The fans saw the game seesaw back and forth. At the end of the third quarter, the score was 49ers 21, Cowboys 20. In the fourth quarter, a hush fell over Candlestick Park as a San Francisco fumble set up another Dallas touchdown making the score Cowboys 27, 49ers 21.

With the ball on the San Francisco 11-yard line and only 4:54 left to play, Montana took command. At the two-minute warning, his team was on the Dallas 49-yard line. With only 1:15 left to play and the ball on the Dallas 13-yard line, Montana called a pass play. He was flushed out of the pocket before he could find an open receiver. He backpedaled a couple of steps and caught a glimpse of wide receiver Dwight Clark in the end zone. Montana was tackled just as he threw the football.

As Clark jumped for the ball, it hit his hands. He juggled it, but he managed to catch it just before it reached the ground. Candlestick Park erupted with cheers. The 49ers had won the game and were going to the Super Bowl.

After the game, Clark said, "I thought I had jumped too soon. I thought I had missed. It hit my hand and I juggled it. But I caught it on the way down."[1] That incredible reception will always be remembered as the Catch.

Super Bowl XVI

On January 24, 1982, the 49ers met the Bengals in Super Bowl XVI. It was the first time either team had made it to the Super Bowl. The 49ers had a great first half and led, 20–0.

After the game, Keena Turner, linebacker for the 49ers, said, "Cincinnati came out fired up in the second half and we definitely lost our momentum at that point."[2] Late in the third quarter, with the Bengals trailing 20–7, a goal-line stand occurred. Cincinnati had the ball first and goal on the San Francisco 3-yard line. On the first play, the Bengals ran left for two yards. On second down and one yard to go, the Bengals ran the ball left, this time for no gain. On third and one, Ken Anderson passed to Charles Alexander for no gain. On fourth and one, Alexander was stopped

The San Francisco 49ers Football Team

*S*an Francisco tight end Charle Young makes a catch during Super Bowl XVI. Jim LeClair (fifty-five) and Bo Harris of the Bengals make the stop.

by 49ers linebacker Dan Bunz while Alexander was trying to dive right. The 49ers had held the Bengals on four tries. Their great effort is remembered by many fans as the most famous goal-line stand in Super Bowl history. The final score was 26–21, and the San Francisco 49ers were the champs.

"Everyone was pretty hyped up in that huddle," defensive end Fred Dean said after the game. "My feeling was, we either stop them here and be the

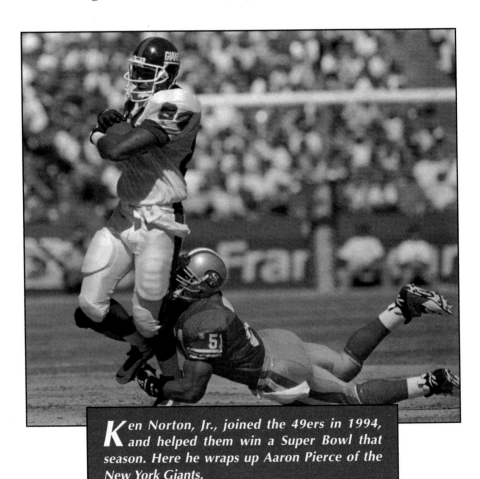

Ken Norton, Jr., joined the 49ers in 1994, and helped them win a Super Bowl that season. Here he wraps up Aaron Pierce of the New York Giants.

The San Francisco 49ers Football Team

champs or we could lose it and think about it for the rest of our lives."[3]

Super Bowl XXIX

During Super Bowl XXIX, Jerry Rice had a sinus infection, and twice throughout the game he received fluids intravenously. However, on the third play of the game he beat his defenders and raced down the middle for a 44-yard touchdown pass. It had taken 1 minute and 24 seconds for the 49ers to score. The connection of Young to Rice had made Super Bowl history by scoring the quickest touchdown in any Super Bowl.

Later in the first quarter, Rice separated his shoulder, but he went out of the game for only one series of plays. The game marked Rice's third Super Bowl appearance. He now held Super Bowl records for most career receiving yards (512), most career points (42), most career receptions (28), and most career touchdowns (17). The 49ers had defeated the San Diego Chargers, 49–26.

When asked about his injury, Rice said, "I felt I couldn't let my team down. I felt that as long as I was on the football field, I was a threat."[4]

Steve Mariucci was hired as head coach of the 49ers in 1997. He led them to a Western Division championship in his first season.

6

PROMISING FUTURE

The future looks bright for the San Francisco 49ers and their fans. On January 22, 1997, after the resignation of George Seifert, the 49ers signed Steve Mariucci as their new head coach, the team's thirteenth. Mariucci came to San Francisco with an excellent coaching background. In 1985, he coached with the Los Angeles Rams for a short time. After that, he successfully coached at several colleges. In 1992, he became quarterbacks coach for the Green Bay Packers. He remained at that position for four years. He was head coach for one year at the University of California before joining the 49ers.

Home Field

From 1946 to 1970, the San Francisco 49ers played their games in Kezar Stadium. Since 1971, their home games have been played in Candlestick Park. In 1995, the park's name was changed to 3Com Park, and the stadium was expanded. It presently holds 70,207 fans, and the playing surface of 3Com Park is natural grass.

The San Francisco fans have an exciting event in their future. They await the completion and opening of their new stadium. On June 3, 1997, the voters of the city showed their love for the 49ers and made sure that the team would stay in San Francisco.

Rumors began to circulate near the end of the 1998 season about a possible coaching change. The rumors were put to a quick end. Mariucci, with a record of 26–9, including the playoffs, still had three years left on his original contract. To show their approval of Coach Mariucci and his record, the 49ers signed him to a new five-year contract.

Acting president of the team Larry Thrailkill said, "Steve Mariucci is our football coach. We're not looking for anyone else to coach our team."[1]

Front Office Moves

At the end of the 1998 season, the organization did make several personnel changes. Bill Walsh, who successfully coached the 49ers to three Super Bowl titles, was appointed general manager. His first major decision was to hire former UCLA coach Terry Donahue as director of player personnel. Walsh and Donahue, together with John McVay, the director of football operations, hope to help the 49ers become Super Bowl winners again.

Gold Stars

After the 49ers signed running back Garrison Hearst, Coach Mariucci stated, "As he gets more and more comfortable in our offense, he is going to become extremely dangerous."[2]

Of his talented pass receiver, Coach Mariucci said, "I always felt that Jerry [Rice] was the best receiver of all time. He's not only exceptional on game days, but he's equally exceptional every day in practice. He works harder than anyone and his conditioning is legendary."[3]

Their future Hall of Fame quarterback, Steve Young, is one of the best in the league. Mariucci said of his famous quarterback, "Steve [Young] is very determined to play for several more years. He feels he's in

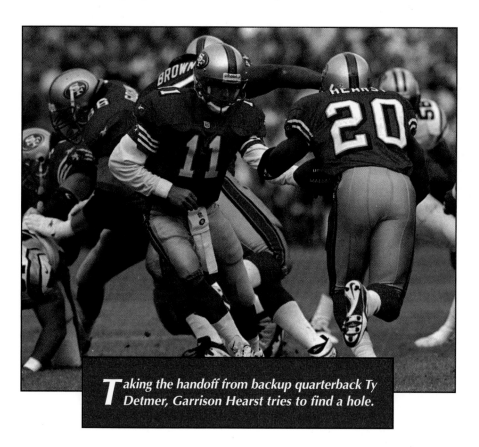

Taking the handoff from backup quarterback Ty Detmer, Garrison Hearst tries to find a hole.

*B*ryant Young sacks Vikings quarterback Jeff George. Young was the 49ers best defensive player in the late 1990s.

the prime of his life and the prime of his career. I believe he still has some of his best years in front of him."[4]

Another bright spot is defensive left tackle Bryant Young. Young was drafted by the 49ers in 1994, and earned NFL Defensive Rookie of the Year honors. He continued to play outstanding football until suffering a broken leg on December 3, 1998. He returned to play sooner than expected in 1999 and finished the season with 11 sacks.

Coach Mariucci and the San Francisco fans are depending on the team's many talented players to bring the Vince Lombardi Trophy back to their city very soon.

STATISTICS

The 49ers History

SEASONS	W	L	T	PCT.	PLAYOFFS	CHAMPIONSHIPS
1946–49*	38	14	2	.722	1–1	None
1950–59	63	54	3	.538	0–1	None
1960–69	57	74	7	.438	—	None
1970–79	60	82	2	.424	2–3	NFC Western Division, 1970–72
1980–89	104	47	1	.688	13–4	Super Bowl XVI, XIX, XXIII, XXIV NFC Western Division, 1981, 1983–84, 1986–89
1990–99	113	47	0	.706	8–7	Super Bowl XXIX NFC Western Division, 1990, 1992–95, 1997

*The 49ers were part of the All-America Football Conference from 1946 to 1949.

W=Wins   **L**=Losses   **T**=Ties
PCT.=Winning Percentage   **PLAYOFFS**=Playoff Record

The 49ers Today

YEAR	W	L	PCT.	COACH	DIVISION FINISH
1990	14	2	.875	George Seifert	1st
1991	10	6	.625	George Seifert	3rd
1992	14	2	.875	George Seifert	1st
1993	10	6	.625	George Seifert	1st
1994	13	3	.813	George Seifert	1st
1995	11	5	.688	George Seifert	1st
1996	12	4	.750	George Seifert	2nd
1997	13	3	.813	Steve Mariucci	1st

The San Francisco 49ers Football Team

The 49ers Today (continued)

YEAR	W	L	PCT.	COACH	DIVISION FINISH
1998	12	4	.750	Steve Mariucci	2nd
1999	4	12	.250	Steve Mariucci	4th

Total History

W	L	T	PCT.	SUPER BOWL WINS
435	318	15	.576	5

Coaching Records

COACH	YEARS COACHED	RECORD	CHAMPIONSHIPS
Lawrence "Buck" Shaw*	1946–54	71–39–4	None
Red Strader	1955	4–8	None
Frankie Albert	1956–58	19–16–1	None
Red Hickey	1959–63	27–27–1	None
Jack Christiansen	1963–67	26–38–3	None
Dick Nolan	1968–75	54–53–5	NFC Western Division, 1970–72
Monte Clark	1976	8–6	None
Ken Meyer	1977	5–9	None
Pete McCulley	1978	1–8	None
Fred O'Connor	1978	1–6	None
Bill Walsh	1979–88	92–59–1	Super Bowl XVI, XIX, XXIII NFC Western Division, 1981, 1983–84, 1986–88
George Seifert	1989–96	98–30	Super Bowl XXIV, XXIX NFC Western Division, 1989–90, 1992–95
Steve Mariucci	1997–99	29–19	NFC Western Division, 1997

*Includes statistics from All-America Football Conference.
Chart includes only regular season won/lost records.

Great 49ers Career Statistics

PASSING

PLAYER	SEASONS	Y	G	ATT	COMP	YDS	TD
Joe Montana[H]	1979–92	15	192	5,391	3,409	40,551	273
Y. A. Tittle*[H]	1951–60	15	176	3,817	2,118	28,339	212
Steve Young**	1987–98	15	169	4,149	2,667	33,124	232

RUSHING

PLAYER	SEASONS	Y	G	ATT	YDS	AVG	TD
Roger Craig	1983–90	11	165	1,991	8,189	4.1	73
Garrison Hearst	1997–98	6	74	1,166	4,939	4.2	20
Hugh McElhenny[H]	1952–60	13	143	1,124	5,281	4.7	38
Joe Perry*[H]	1948–49	2	25	192	1,345	7.0	18
	1950–60, 1963	14	153	1,737	8,378	4.8	53

RECEIVING

PLAYER	SEASONS	Y	G	REC	YDS	AVG	TD
Dwight Clark	1979–87	9	134	506	6,750	13.3	48
Jerry Rice	1985–98	15	221	1,200	18,299	15.2	180

DEFENSE

PLAYER	SEASONS	Y	G	ACCOMPLISHMENTS
Leo Nomellini[H]	1950–63	14	174	Played in 174 consecutive games.
Ronnie Lott[H]	1981–90	14	192	63 career interceptions; played in 10 Pro Bowls as a safety.

SEASONS=Seasons with 49ers   ATT=Attempts   TD=Touchdowns
Y=Years in NFL   COMP=Completions   AVG=Average
G=Games   YDS=Yards   REC=Receptions

*Includes statistics from All-America Football Conference.
**Steve Young also played professionally in the United States Football League. Those statistics are not included.
[H] Hall of Fame member

The San Francisco 49ers Football Team

CHAPTER NOTES

Chapter 1. Super Bowl XXIII

1. Jerry Green, *Super Bowl Chronicles* (Grand Rapids, Mich.: Masters Press, 1991), p. 301.

2. Brian White, "Bad Break: Krumrie Injury Weakens Bengals," *The Green Bay Press Gazette*, January 23, 1989, p. C1.

3. Mike Blanchl, "Rice Dances to MVP Despite Bum Ankle," *The Green Bay Press Gazette*, January 23, 1989, p. C2.

4. Green, p. 302.

Chapter 2. An Exciting History

1. Michael W. Tuckman and Jeff Schultz, *The San Francisco 49ers: Team of the Decade* (Rocklin, Calif.: Prima Publishing & Communications, 1989), p. 190.

2. Michael L. LaBlanc, *Football Professional Sports Team Histories* (Detroit, Mich.: Gale Research Inc., 1994), p. 504.

3. Ibid.

4. Ibid., p. 505.

Chapter 3. Star Players

1. Tony Canadeo, personal interview with author, August 20, 1998.

2. Dennis J. Harrington, *The Pro Football Hall of Fame* (Jefferson, N.C.: McFarland & Company, Inc., Publishers, 1991), p. 146.

3. Bob Carroll, ed., *Total Football* (New York: HarperCollins Publishers, 1997), p. 265.

4. Pat Haden, *The 1997 San Francisco 49er Media Guide* (New Washington, Ohio: The Herald Printing Company, 1997), p. 391.

5. "Steve Young," *Current Biography Yearbook*, Fifty-fourth Annual Cumulation (New York: H. W. Wilson Company, 1993), p. 614.

6. Ibid.

Chapter 4. Building the Team

1. Beau Riffenburgh, ed., *The Official NFL Encyclopedia*, 4th edition (New York: New American Library, 1986), p. 169.

2. Michael W. Tuckman and Jeff Schultz, *The San Francisco 49ers Team of the Decade* (Rocklin, Calif.: Prima Publishing & Communications, 1989), p. 190.

3. Ray Didinger, *Game Plans for Success* (Boston, Mass.: Little Brown and Company, 1995), p. 171.

4. Ibid., p. 192.

Chapter 5. Thrilling Moments

1. Michael W. Tuckman and Jeff Schultz, *The San Francisco 49ers Team of the Decade* (Rocklin, Calif.: Prima Publishing & Communications, 1989), p.139.

2. Ibid., p. 144.

3. Ibid., p. 145.

4. Hank Gola, "Rice Fights Pain, But Feels Joy," *The Green Bay Press Gazette*, January 30, 1995, p. C3.

Chapter 6. Promising Future

1. Michael Silver, "Eye Catching," *Sports Illustrated*, January 11, 1999, p. 46.

2. Steve Mariucci, *The 1997 San Francisco 49ers Media Guide* (New Washington, Ohio: The Herald Printing Company, 1997), p. 390.

3. Ibid., p. 391.

4. Ibid.

GLOSSARY

AAFC—The All-America Football Conference, a separate football league from 1946 to 1949.

AFC—The teams in the American Football Conference.

contract—A written agreement between two parties, such as between a player or a coach and a football organization.

draft picks—Players chosen by teams from the college ranks. Usually draft picks are college seniors, but occasionally they are drafted after their junior year in college.

merger—A combination of two or more organizations.

NFC—The teams in the National Football Conference.

NFL—The National Football League. The NFL is made up of the teams in the AFC and the NFC.

Pro Bowl—An all-star game played after the Super Bowl. It is made up of the top players from both the AFC and the NFC.

Pro Football Hall of Fame—A building in Canton, Ohio, where the greatest football players are showcased.

rookie—A player playing his first year in the NFL.

Super Bowl—The National Football League championship game played between the winners of the AFC and the NFC playoffs.

Vince Lombardi Trophy—The trophy awarded to the team that wins the Super Bowl.

FURTHER READING

Dickey, Glenn. *Sports Great Jerry Rice*. Hillside, N.J.: Enslow Publishers, Inc., 1993.

Duden, Jane. *The Super Bowl*. Parsippany, N.J.: Silver Burdett Press, 1992.

Dunnahoo, Terry Janson, and Herma Silverstein. *Pro Football: The Halls of Fame*. New York: Crestwood House, 1994.

Gutman, Bill. *Steve Young, NFL Passing Wizard*. Brookfield, Conn.: Millbrook Press, Inc., 1996.

Kavanagh, Jack. *Sports Great Joe Montana*. Hillside, N.J.: Enslow Publishers, Inc., 1992.

Knapp, Ron. *Steve Young: Star Quarterback*. Springfield, N.J.: Enslow Publishers, Inc., 1996.

Lace, William W. *Top 10 Football Quarterbacks*. Hillside, N.J.: Enslow Publishers, Inc., 1994.

Raber, Thomas. *Joe Montana: Comeback Quarterback*. Minneapolis, Minn.: The Lerner Publishing Group, 1989.

Raffo, Dave. *Football*. Austin, Tex.: Raintree Steck Vaughn, 1994.

Rothaus, James R. *The San Francisco 49ers*. Mankato, Minn.: Creative Education, 1986.

Savage, Jeff. *Top 10 Professional Football Coaches*. Springfield, N.J.: Enslow Publishers, Inc., 1998.

Spence, Jim. *Joe Montana: The Comeback Kid*. Vero Beach, Fla.: The Rourke Press, Inc., 1995.

Young, Steve, and Greg Brown. *Forever Young*. Dallas, Tex.: Taylor Publishing Co., 1996.

INDEX

WHERE TO WRITE

San Francisco 49ers
4949 Centennial Boulevard
Santa Clara, CA 95054-1229

WEB SITES

http://www.sf49ers.com
http://www.nfl.com/49ers